TRINITY
COLLEGE LONDON PRESS

T0088291

GRADE

02
BASS

Published by
Trinity College London Press Ltd.
trinitycollege.com

Registered in England
Company no. 09726123

Photography by Zute Lightfoot, lightfootphoto.com

Printed in England by Caligraving Ltd.

THE EXAM AT A GLANCE

In your exam you will perform a set of three songs and one of the session skills assessments. You can choose the order of your set list.

SONG 1

Choose a song from this book.

SONG 2

Choose *either* a different song from this book
or a song from the list of additional Trinity Rock & Pop arrangements, available at trinityrock.com
or a song you have chosen yourself: this could be your own cover version or a song that you have written. It should be at the same level as the songs in this book and match the parameters at trinityrock.com

SONG 3: TECHNICAL FOCUS

Song 3 is designed to help you develop specific and relevant techniques in performance. Choose one of the technical focus songs from this book, which cover two specific technical elements.

SESSION SKILLS

Choose *either* **playback** *or* **improvising**.

Session skills are an essential part of every Rock & Pop exam. They are designed to help you develop the techniques music industry performers need.

Sample tests are available in our *Session Skills* books and free examples can be downloaded from trinityrock.com

ACCESS ALL AREAS

GET THE FULL ROCK & POP EXPERIENCE ONLINE AT TRINITYROCK.COM

We have created a range of digital resources to support your learning and give you insider information from the music industry, available online. You will find support, advice and digital content on:

- Songs, performance and technique
- Session skills
- The music industry

You can access tips and tricks from industry professionals featuring:

- Bite-sized videos that include tips from professional musicians on techniques used in the songs
- 'Producer's notes' on the tracks, to increase your knowledge of rock and pop
- Blog posts on performance tips, musical styles, developing technique and advice from the music industry

JOIN US ONLINE AT:

 /TRINITYROCKANDPOP    @TRINITY_ROCK    /TRINITYROCKANDPOP   and at **TRINITYROCK.COM**

CONTENTS

THE AUDIO

Professional demo & backing tracks can be downloaded free, see inside cover for details.

Music preparation and book layout by Andrew Skirrow for Camden Music Services
Music consultants: Nick Crispin, Chris Walters, Christopher Hussey, Mike Mansbridge
Audio arranged, recorded & produced by Tom Fleming
Bass arrangements by Sam Burgess & Ben Heartland

Musicians
Bass: Sam Burgess
Drums: George Double
Guitar: Tom Fleming
Cello & Spoken Vocal: Sophie Gledhill
Vocals: Bo Walton, Alison Symons, Brendan Reilly

YOUR
PAGE
NOTES

TECHNICAL FOCUS

BROWN EYED GIRL VAN MORRISON

WORDS AND MUSIC: VAN MORRISON

SINGLE BY
Van Morrison

ALBUM
Blowin' Your Mind

B-SIDE
Goodbye Baby

RELEASED
June 1967

LABEL
Bang

WRITER
Van Morrison

PRODUCER
Bert Berns

Born in Belfast, Northern Ireland, Van Morrison fronted the rock'n'roll band Them in the mid-60s before embarking upon a prolific and enduring solo career of continuing success. In 2015 he was awarded the highest honour at the Songwriters Hall of Fame for his body of outstanding creative work.

Morrison's debut solo single 'Brown Eyed Girl' was released in 1967, a year after Them split up. This infectiously catchy and summery number launched Morrison's career in the US, where the single reached No. 10. The female backing vocals were performed by The Sweet Inspirations (featuring Whitney Houston's mother Cissy), who can also be heard on Aretha Franklin's 'Chain of Fools' and Jimi Hendrix's 'Burning of the Midnight Lamp', as well as backing Elvis Presley from 1969 until his death. In 2011, 'Brown Eyed Girl' was honoured for having received more than 10 million plays on US radio, making it one of the most played songs in history. But despite its enduring popularity, its success always baffled Morrison: 'It's not one of my best. I mean, I've got about 300 songs that I think are better.'

TECHNICAL FOCUS

Two technical elements are featured in this song:

- Note lengths
- Rhythmic accuracy

There are a range of different **note lengths** and rests in this bass part. Make sure these are accurate, as the rests and silences play an important part in creating the groove. Related to this is **rhythmic accuracy**, and there is a lot of rhythmic detail in all sections of this song to pay careful attention to.

BROWN EYED GIRL

WORDS AND MUSIC: VAN MORRISON

Intro

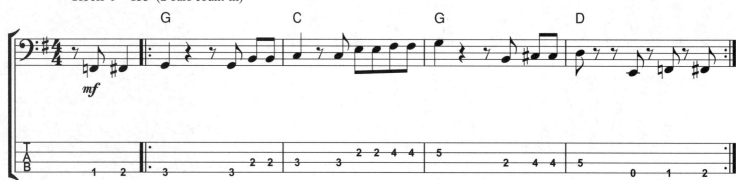

Verse

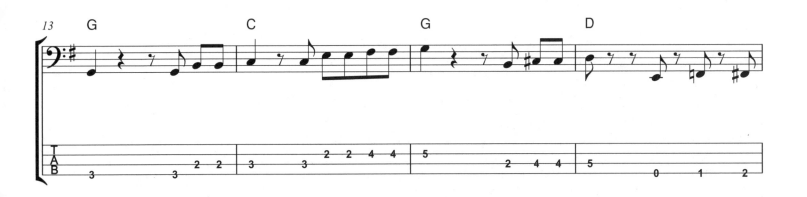

Pre-Chorus

Chorus

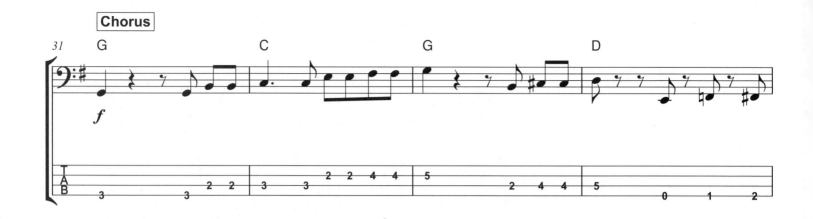

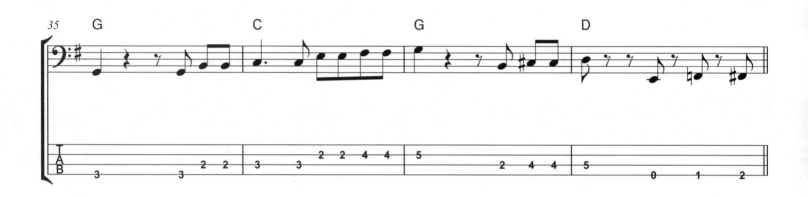

Outro

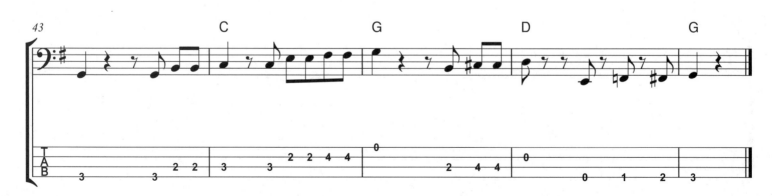

DON'T WANNA FIGHT
ALABAMA SHAKES

WORDS AND MUSIC: ALABAMA SHAKES

SINGLE BY
Alabama Shakes

ALBUM
Sound & Color

RELEASED
10 February 2015

LABEL
ATO (USA)
Rough Trade (UK)

WRITER
Alabama Shakes

PRODUCER
Blake Mills

Alabama Shakes formed in 2009 with a blend of fiery blues-rock and hard-hitting Southern soul, quickly bringing them international attention. With a formidable live reputation and two hit albums they have become one of the biggest bands to emerge in the 2010s.

'Don't Wanna Fight' was the first taste of Alabama Shakes' second album, 2015's US chart-topper *Sound & Color*. An electrifying mix of funky guitar riffs, soulful bass, chunky drums and the passionately raspy vocal performance of singer Brittany Howard, the impressive track expanded the band's range into more diverse, genre-bending territory. Likening the singer's opening howl to a hurricane, *Rolling Stone* magazine wrote, 'After reintroducing herself with a spine-tingling squeal, singer-guitarist Brittany Howard goes on to deliver a dizzying vocal performance that splits the difference between James Brown and Barry Gibb.' The song received two Grammy Awards in February 2016 for Best Rock Song and Best Rock Performance, with *Sound & Color* also picking up the Best Alternative Music Album honour.

⚡ PERFORMANCE TIPS

The characteristic riff of this song is given to the bass in the verse, so aim to play this with energy and precision. Elsewhere this is a varied and interesting bass part with feature moments in bars 12, 25, 35 and 37 and occasional slides to look out for.

DON'T WANNA FIGHT

WORDS AND MUSIC: ALABAMA SHAKES

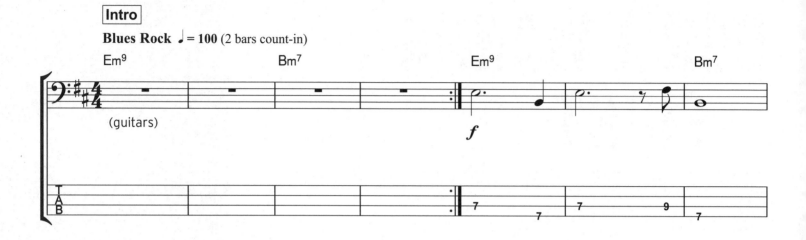

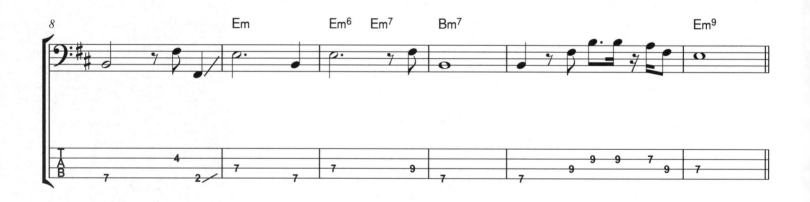

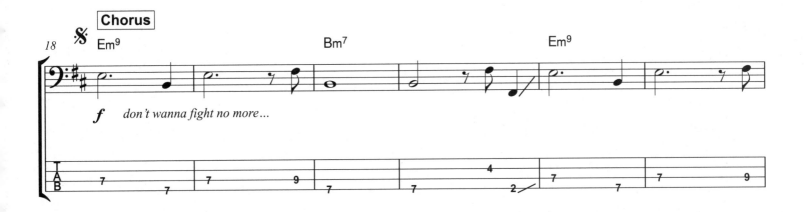

Chorus

f   *don't wanna fight no more...*

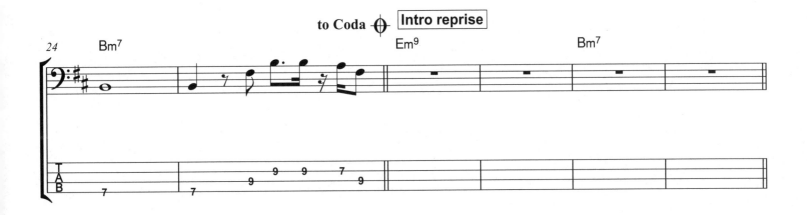

to Coda ✛ **Intro reprise**

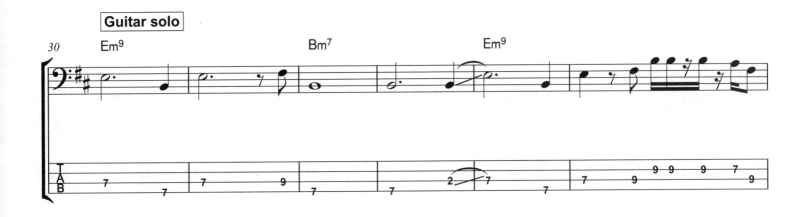

Guitar solo

D.S. al Coda

✛ **Coda**

YOUR
PAGE
NOTES

KNOCK ON WOOD
EDDIE FLOYD

WORDS AND MUSIC: EDDIE FLOYD, STEVE CROPPER

SINGLE BY
Eddie Floyd

ALBUM
Knock on Wood

B-SIDE
Got to Make a Comeback

RELEASED
September 1966

RECORDED
July-December 1966
Stax Recording Studios
Memphis, Tennessee USA

LABEL
Stax Records

WRITERS
Eddie Floyd
Steve Cropper

PRODUCER
Steve Cropper

A founder member of Detroit vocal group The Falcons, Eddie Floyd moved to Memphis, Tennessee in 1965 as a staff songwriter for the legendary Stax Records. Early success came in collaboration with Booker T & The MGs' guitarist Steve Cropper, the pair responsible for the Wilson Pickett hit '634-5789'.

Floyd and Cropper wrote 'Knock on Wood' with Otis Redding in mind, though it would become the launching point for Floyd's enduring solo career. The weather in Memphis proved a source of inspiration: 'It's like thunder, lightning, the way you love me is frightening' (composed in the Lorraine Motel, where Martin Luther King was assassinated two years later). 'Knock on Wood' has been described as the archetypal Stax record and the peak of 60s soul, hitting No. 1 on the US R&B chart in 1966. Redding did record a hit version of the song with Carla Thomas for their 1967 duets album *King & Queen*. A disco version by Amii Stewart was the most successful, reaching No. 1 in the US and No. 6 in the UK in 1979.

⚡ PERFORMANCE TIPS

This satisfying bass part contains a few different elements to keep you busy. The repeated quavers in the intro need to be played evenly, but notice how they also pick out the notes of the riff played by the horns. The rhythm in the verse needs a relaxed, grooving feel before the return of the repeated quavers at the chorus. The three-bar crescendo starting at bar 26 needs to be evenly distributed across its full duration.

KNOCK ON WOOD

WORDS AND MUSIC:
EDDIE FLOYD, STEVE CROPPER

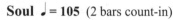

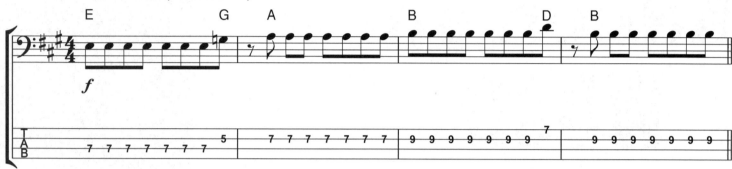

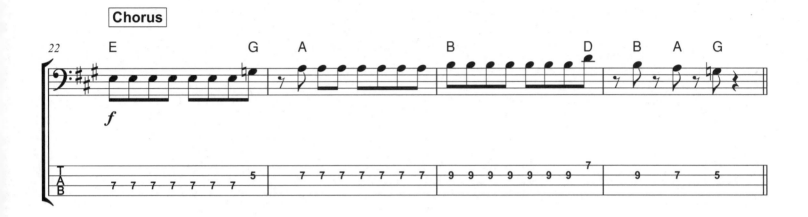

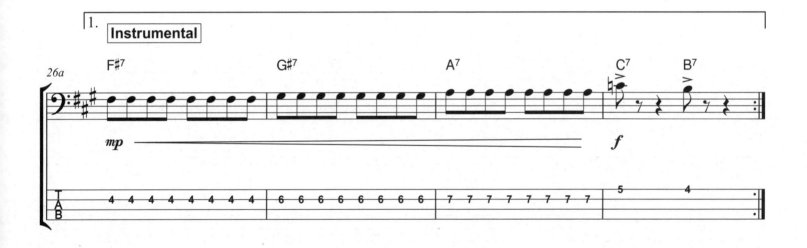

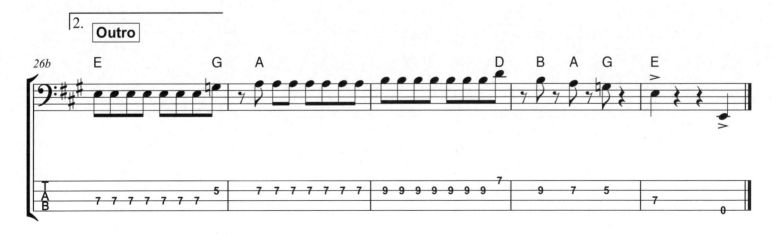

YOUR
PAGE
NOTES

PRIVATE LIFE
GRACE JONES

WORDS AND MUSIC: CHRISSIE HYNDE

SINGLE BY
Grace Jones

ALBUM
Warm Leatherette

B-SIDE
She's Lost Control

RELEASED
9 May 1980 (album)
27 June 1980 (single)

RECORDED
1979-1980

LABEL
Island

WRITERS
Chrissie Hynde

PRODUCERS
Chris Blackwell
Alex Sadkin

With her towering height, androgynous looks, incredible style and fearless attitude, Grace Jones is one of the most iconic figures in popular music. Taking in reggae, R&B, synth-pop and funk, her career has endured from the disco era of the 1970s through to headlining dance music festivals in the 2010s.

'Private Life' was written by Chrissie Hynde and originally recorded by the Pretenders for their eponymously titled 1980 debut album. Within months, Jones, at the suggestion of Island label boss Chris Blackwell, recorded her version of the song for her fourth album, *Warm Leatherette*, at Compass Point Studios in the Bahamas. The album was produced by Alex Sadkin, who had produced Bob Marley and the Wailers' *Survival* album the year before, and featured the distinctive sound of Sly and Robbie on bass and drums. This legendary rhythm section and production duo are one of music's most prolific outfits, with over 50,000 recording credits to their name. Hynde said of Jones's version:

> Like all the other London punks I wanted to do reggae, and I wrote 'Private Life'. When I first heard Grace's version I thought, 'Now that's how it's supposed to sound!'

⚡ PERFORMANCE TIPS

This song is all about the repeated riff, which makes up most of the bass part. There are some changes of dynamic, but otherwise, aim for a consistent, even, driving effect. Go for a feeling of falling off the notes in bars 18 and 38, where slides are used but with no particular note to head for. Look out for other, smaller slides too.

PRIVATE LIFE

WORDS AND MUSIC: CHRISSIE HYNDE

New wave reggae ♩ = 132
(2 bar count-in)

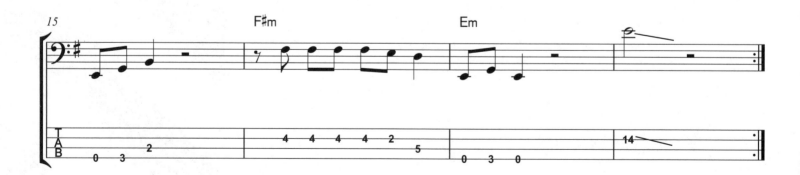

YOUR
PAGE
NOTES

SINGLE BY
Badly Drawn Boy

ALBUM
About a Boy

B-SIDE
Walk in the Park with Angie

Hamster Countdown

Something to Talk About

RELEASED
8 April 2002 (album)
10 June 2002 (single)

RECORDED
2001
Larrabee East, Third Stone
Recording & Cello Studios
Los Angeles, California,
USA

AIR Studios, London
England (album)

LABEL
Twisted Nerve
XL Recordings

WRITER
Damon Gough

PRODUCERS
Badly Drawn Boy
Tom Rothrock

TECHNICAL FOCUS

SOMETHING TO TALK ABOUT
BADLY DRAWN BOY

WORDS AND MUSIC: DAMON GOUGH

Badly Drawn Boy is the stage name of Manchester singer-songwriter Damon Gough, whose debut 2000 album *The Hour of Bewilderbeast* won that year's Mercury Music Prize. The album caught the attention of British author Nick Hornby, who asked Gough to score the film adaptation of his novel *About a Boy*.

Taken from the soundtrack to *About a Boy,* a 2002 comedy starring Hugh Grant and a 12-year-old Nicholas Hoult, 'Something to Talk About' was the second single to be released from the No. 6 UK hit album. The album was produced and mixed by Tom Rothrock, who had worked on the commercial breakthrough albums by two American artists often compared at the time with Badly Drawn Boy: Elliott Smith and Beck. Joey Waronker, who played drums on albums by both Beck and Elliott Smith, also plays drums on 'Something to Talk About' (as well as the album's first single 'Silent Sigh'). Two months after the soundtrack's release, 'Something to Talk About' reached No. 28 on the UK singles chart.

TECHNICAL FOCUS

Two technical elements are featured in this song:

- Slides
- Rests

Slides are a big feature of this song, so emphasise them where they occur.
Rests are used in some passages to create contrast with other legato sections. Observe the rests carefully to bring out these contrasts.

SOMETHING TO TALK ABOUT

WORDS AND MUSIC: DAMON GOUGH

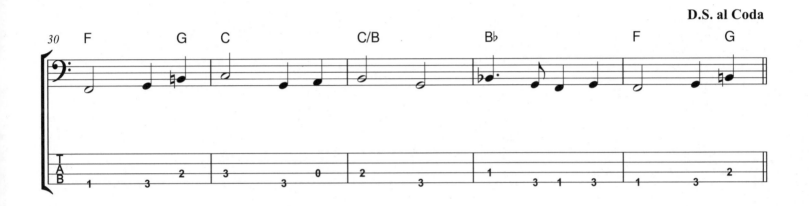

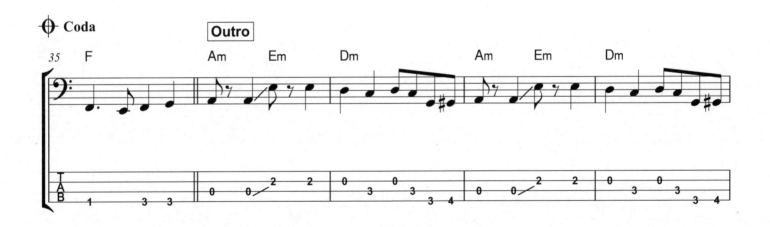

YOUR
PAGE
NOTES

SHE SELLS SANCTUARY

THE CULT

WORDS AND MUSIC: IAN ASTBURY, BILLY DUFFY

SINGLE BY
The Cult

ALBUM
Love

B-SIDE
No. 13

RELEASED
17 May 1985

RECORDED
**11-15 March 1985
Olympic Studios
London, England**

LABEL
Beggars Banquet

WRITERS
**Ian Astbury
Billy Duffy**

PRODUCER
Steve Brown

Following the demise of his early-80s band Southern Death Cult, singer Ian Astbury joined forces with guitarist Billy Duffy to form Death Cult before finalising their name as The Cult in 1984. Inspired by Led Zeppelin and The Doors, their finely honed hard rock sound has yielded a successful career, still going strong after more than 30 years.

'She Sells Sanctuary' was released in May 1985 and climbed to No. 15 in the UK within three months. It was the first single to be released from their top-five hit album Love and the last song to be recorded with drummer Nigel Preston who was replaced by Mark Brzezicki of Big Country. Its distinctive sound came about after Duffy found a violin bow in the studio and 'started to play the guitar with the bow like Jimmy Page. I just hit every pedal I had on the pedal board. Then once I stopped banging the strings I played the middle section of the song, which was kind of a pick thing with all the BOSS pedals on, and that sound just leaped out. The producer went, "Hold it, that's great!" and we decided to start the song with that mystical sound. If I hadn't found that violin bow lying around, we wouldn't have gone there.'

⚡ PERFORMANCE TIPS

For the bass, this song is an exercise in evenness and consistency. The driving quavers and crotchets help create a feeling of forward momentum that lets up only in the breakdown section, where you'll need to count carefully to ensure that your long notes last their correct duration. Elsewhere, look out for the long slides and play these with confidence.

SHE SELLS SANCTUARY

WORDS AND MUSIC:
IAN ASTBURY, BILLY DUFFY

YOUR
PAGE
NOTES

SINGLE BY
The Temper Trap

ALBUM
Conditions

B-SIDE
Little Boy

RELEASED
16 September 2008

RECORDED
**2008, Sing Sing Studios
Melbourne, Australia**

**March 2009
Assault & Battery 2
London, England (album)**

LABEL
**Liberation
Infectious Records
Glassnote Records**

WRITERS
**Dougy Mandagi
Lorenzo Silitto**

PRODUCER
Jim Abbiss

TECHNICAL FOCUS

SWEET DISPOSITION
THE TEMPER TRAP

WORDS AND MUSIC: DOUGY MANDAGI, LORENZO SILITTO

Formed in 2005 in Melbourne, Australia by Indonesian-born singer and guitarist Dougy Mandagi, lead guitarist Lorenzo Sillitto, bassist Jonathon Aherne and drummer Toby Dundas, The Temper Trap have released three albums between 2009 and 2016, two of which have topped the Australian chart.

'Sweet Disposition' was the debut single by The Temper Trap and an immediate breakthrough international hit. Written by Mandagi and Sillitto and taken from their debut album *Conditions*, this soaring, anthemic song reached No. 6 on the UK singles chart in October 2009, shortly after its appearance in the hit American romantic comedy *500 Days of Summer*. Although only peaking at No. 14 in the band's native Australia, 'Sweet Disposition' would go on to win two prestigious prizes there in 2001: Most Popular Australian Single at the ARIA (Australian Recording Industry Association) Awards and Song of the Year at the APRA (Australasian Performing Right Association) Music Awards.

TECHNICAL FOCUS

Two technical elements are featured in this song:

- Rhythm
- Dynamics

The **rhythm** of the opening motif needs to be played with precision, and you'll need to take care to observe the semiquaver rest. **Dynamics** are used a lot, including long crescendos and diminuendos, which will need to be carefully and evenly gradated.

SWEET DISPOSITION

WORDS AND MUSIC:
DOUGY MANDAGI, LORENZO SILITTO

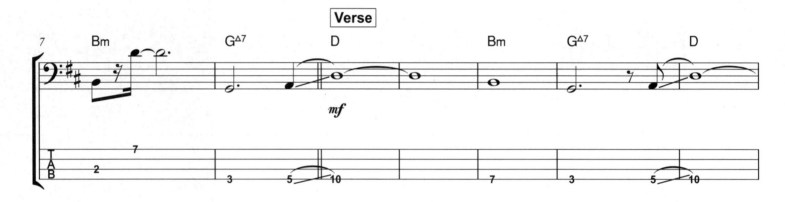

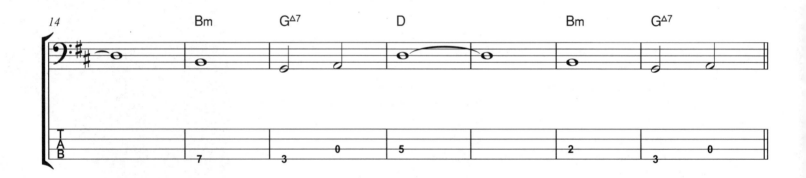

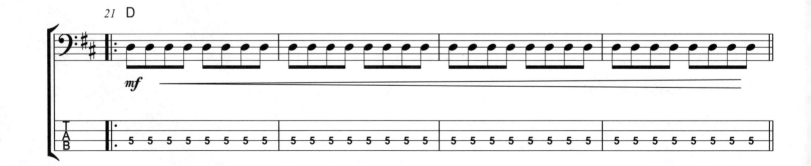

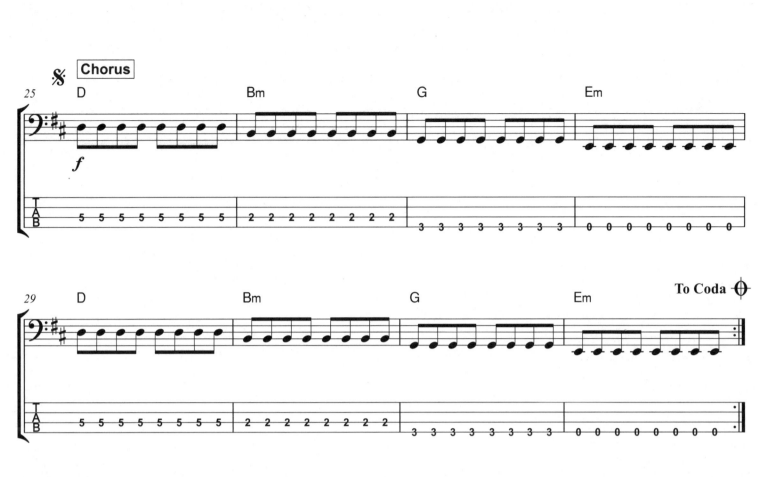

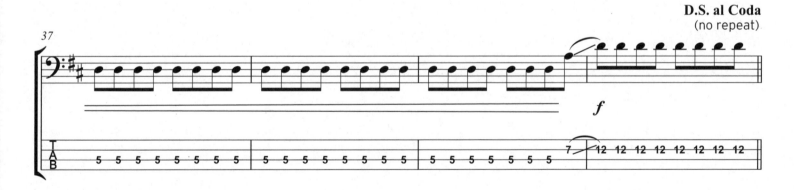

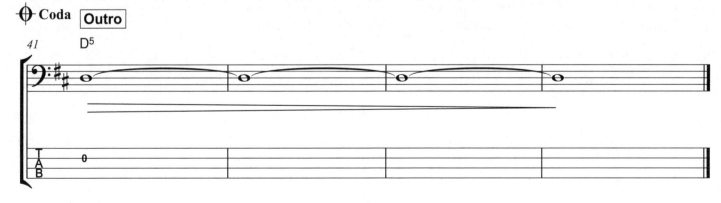

YOUR
PAGE
NOTES

YOU'VE GOT A FRIEND

CAROLE KING

WORDS AND MUSIC: CAROLE KING

SINGLE BY
Carole King

ALBUM
Tapestry

RELEASED
10 February 1971 (album)

RECORDED
**January 1971
A&M Recording Studios
Los Angeles, California
USA**

LABEL
Ode Records

WRITER
Carole King

PRODUCER
Lou Adler

Carole King began her career penning songs with her future husband Gerry Goffin, a songwriting partnership that produced US No. 1s such as 'Will You Still Love Me Tomorrow', 'Take Good Care of My Baby' and 'The Loco-Motion'. Her second solo album, 1971's *Tapestry*, is one of the best-selling albums of all time.

According to King, 'You've Got a Friend' was 'as close to pure inspiration as I've ever experienced. The song wrote itself. It was written by something outside myself, through me.' It was inspired by a line in James Taylor's classic song 'Fire and Rain' from his 1970 album *Sweet Baby James*, which King played piano on. Taylor played guitar on King's first album, 1970's *Writer*, and would do so again on *Tapestry*, including on 'You've Got a Friend'. Taylor's own cover of the song was released as a single a month after the release of *Tapestry*. It reached No. 1 in the US and No. 4 in the UK and won two Grammy Awards including Song of the Year, while *Tapestry* picked up Album of the Year.

⚡ PERFORMANCE TIPS

The bass makes an important contribution to the gentle groove of this song. Look out for feature moments, for example bars 20, 24 and others, where you have a chance to bring out the bassline and play it melodically. There are some subtle dynamic changes too.

YOU'VE GOT A FRIEND

WORDS AND MUSIC: CAROLE KING

Verse

Rock ballad ♩ = 84 (2 bars count-in)

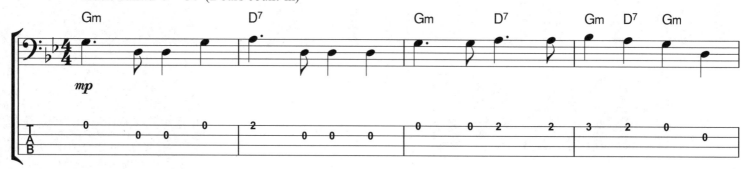

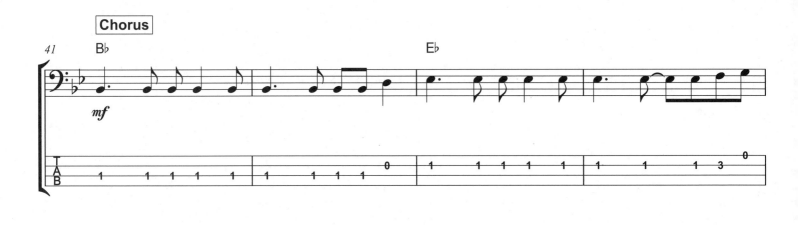

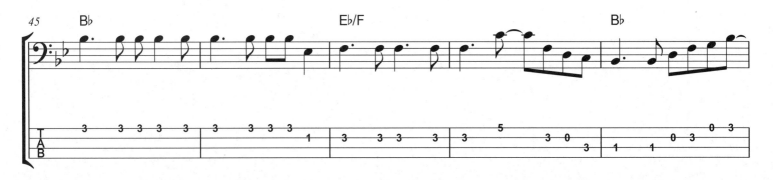

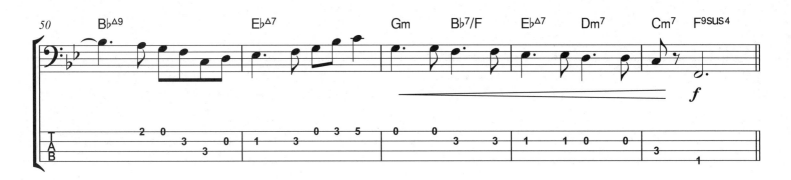

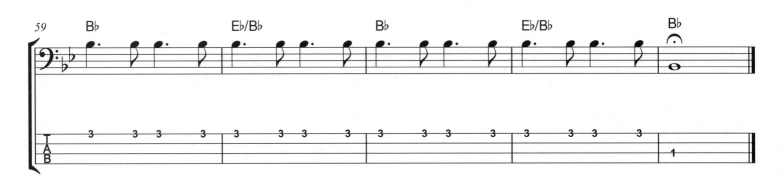

PLAYING WITH BACKING TRACKS

All your backing tracks can be downloaded from soundwise.co.uk

- The backing tracks begin with a click track, which sets the tempo and helps you start accurately

- Be careful to balance the volume of the backing track against your instrument

- Listen carefully to the backing track to ensure that you are playing in time

If you are creating your own backing track, here are some further tips:

- Make sure that the sound quality is of a good standard

- Think carefully about the instruments/sounds you are using on the backing track

- Avoid copying what you are playing in the exam on the backing track – it should support, not duplicate

- Do you need to include a click track at the beginning?

COPYRIGHT IN A SONG

If you are a singer, instrumentalist or songwriter it is important to know about copyright. When someone writes a song they automatically own the copyright (sometimes called 'the rights'). Copyright begins once a piece of music has been documented or recorded (eg by video, CD or score notation) and protects the interests of the creators. This means that others cannot copy it, sell it, make it available online or record it without the owner's permission or the appropriate licence.

COVER VERSIONS

- When an artist creates a new version of a song it is called a 'cover version'

- The majority of songwriters subscribe to licensing agencies, also known as 'collecting societies'. When a songwriter is a member of such an agency, the performing rights to their material are transferred to the agency (this includes cover versions of their songs)

- The agency works on the writer's behalf by issuing licences to performance venues, who report what songs have been played, which in turn means that the songwriter will receive a payment for any songs used

- You can create a cover version of a song and use it in an exam without needing a licence

There are different rules for broadcasting (eg TV, radio, internet), selling or copying (pressing CDs, DVDs etc), and for printed material, and the appropriate licences should be sought out.

CHOOSING SONGS FOR YOUR EXAM

SONG 1

Choose a song from this book.

SONG 2

Choose a song which is:

Either a different song from this book

or from the list of additional Trinity Rock & Pop arrangements, available at trinityrock.com

or from a printed or online source

or your own arrangement

or a song that you have written yourself

You can play Song 2 unaccompanied or with a backing track (minus the bass part). If you like, you can create a backing track yourself (or with friends), add your own vocals, or be accompanied live by another musician.

The level of difficulty and length of the song should be similar to the songs in this book and match the parameters available at trinityrock.com

When choosing a song, think about:

- Does it work on my instrument?
- Are there any technical elements that are too difficult for me? (If so, perhaps save it for when you do the next grade)
- Do I enjoy playing it?
- Does it work with my other songs to create a good set list?

SONG 3: TECHNICAL FOCUS

Song 3 is designed to help you develop specific and relevant techniques in performance. Choose one of the technical focus songs from this book, which cover two specific technical elements.

SHEET MUSIC

If your choice for Song 2 is not from this book, you must provide the examiner with a photocopy. The title, writers of the song and your name should be on the sheet music. You must also bring an original copy of the book, or a download version with proof of purchase, for each song that you perform in the exam.

Your music can be:

- A lead sheet with lyrics, chords and melody line
- A chord chart with lyrics
- A full score using conventional staff notation

YOUR
PAGE
NOTES

YOUR
PAGE
NOTES